FANTASTIC VOYAGE

Amanda Dalton is a poet and playwright. Her first book-length collection, *How to Disappear* (Bloodaxe Books 1999), was shortlisted for the Forward Prize for Best First Collection and she was chosen as a Next Generation Poet in 2004. Her second collection, *Stray*, was published by Bloodaxe in 2012. In 2021 Arc published her experimental chapbook, *30 Poems in 30 Days* and, in 2022, Smith|Doorstop published a pamphlet of two long poems, *Notes on Water*. A version of *Notes on Water* was re-created for two voices and soundscape for BBC Radio 3's *Between the Ears*. Her third full-length collection, *Fantastic Voyage* (Bloodaxe Books, 2024), includes the radio version of *Notes on Water* together with a QR code enabling readers to listen to that recording.

Amanda writes extensively for BBC Radio 4 and 3 including original drama, poetry-dramas, classic adaptations, re-imaginings of film, and lyric essays. Her theatre writing includes commissions with Manchester's Royal Exchange, Sheffield Theatres and Keswick's Theatre By The Lake.

Freelance since 2017, much of her career has been focused on teaching, mentoring and the curation and artistic leadership of innovative cross art-form projects, often in collaboration with other artists and communities. Her website is https://www.amandadalton.co.uk

She lives in Hebden Bridge.

AMANDA DALTON

FANTASTIC
VOYAGE

BLOODAXE BOOKS

ISBN: 978 1 78037 711 7

First published 2024 by
Bloodaxe Books Ltd,
Eastburn,
South Park,
Hexham,
Northumberland NE46 1BS

www.bloodaxebooks.com
For further information about Bloodaxe titles
please visit our website and join our mailing list
or write to the above address for a catalogue.

Supported using public funding by
**ARTS COUNCIL
ENGLAND**

Cover design: Neil Astley & Pamela Robertson-Pearce.

Printed in Great Britain by Bell & Bain Limited, Glasgow, Scotland, on
acid-free paper sourced from mills with FSC chain of custody certification.

CONTENTS

9   Fantastic Voyage

10   Belly

10   Takotsubo

10   Gut

10   A Ghost Story

11   **Look Inside!**

12   When Andrea was 7

13   Auntie Irene says

14   One day I watch

15   Andrea's father

16   One day I ask

17   Mum says Nancy Gardiner

18   Janet Bradley says

19   One day I go for a colonoscopy

20   Peter B says

21   Aged 9, Andrea doesn't know

22   One day, I was sawn in half

23   **Notes on Water**

39   **Haunts and Apparitions**

41   Nights I Squat

42   Magic

44   December 1979

45   Three Hauntings

45   1 *Pelican*

46   2 *Girl in White with Trees*

47   3 *Man Dressed as Bat*

48   Missing

49   The Vegetable Lamb of Tartary

51   like a tree

53   The Possibility of Fog

54   Ten Signs of Possession
54   1 *Superhuman Strength*
55   2 *Knowledge of Previously Unknown Languages or Speaking in Tongues (glossolalia).*
56   3 *Unnatural Body Movements*
57   4 *Appearance of Wounds that Vanish as Quickly as They Appear*
58   5 *Paranormal Capabilities*
59   6 *Living Outside the Rules of Society*
60   7 *Being Persistently Ill, Falling into Heavy Sleep and Vomiting Strange Objects*
61   8 *Being Troubled by Spirits*
62   9 *Being Uncomfortable, Ugly and Violent*
63   10 *Making Sounds and Movements Like an Animal*
64   Aftermath

67   Untitled
68   Fantastic Voyage

70   NOTES
71   ACKNOWLEDGEMENTS

The body is the instrument of our hold on the world

SIMONE DE BEAUVOIR
The Second Sex

GRANT: Wait a minute. They can't shrink me.

CARTER: Our miniaturiser can shrink anything.

GRANT: But I don't want to be miniaturised.

CARTER: It's just for an hour.

GRANT: Not even for a minute.

Fantastic Voyage

Fantastic Voyage

She's at the pictures with her dad or maybe she's at home watching TV with her mum or on her own, and she's shrunk. Wherever she is and whoever she's with, she's definitely shrunk and she's inside the submarine diving at terrific speed through saline, heading straight into a circular abyss. She shuts her eyes and waits to die but when she opens them the submarine is floating in a watery wonderland and Owens says *you may unfasten your belts* so she does. Or maybe she stretches her legs on the old settee or takes a Malteser from the box dad bought at the kiosk and it tips – Maltesers rolling under the seat of the boy in front and the woman in front of him. Or maybe there are no sweets, but the submarine is definitely pulled off course again and her stomach definitely tugs and flips and all this happens at once and she thinks *What if the submarine is inside me?* What if it is? What if it never gets out of her or she never gets out of it? If years from now she's lying on a table watching a screen as cameras prod her gut, her heart, her brain, searching for a miniature child still bathing in extracellular fluid, trapped in a shrunken submarine?

Belly

Lilliputian lost
inside the worm of belly
scouring the crawl space
for a heart feeling the sting
of world through its wormy skin.

Takotsubo

A pot for trapping
oysters or this swollen heart
you have nested in
sac straining under your weight
blood forgetting how to run.

Gut

An oystercatcher
drowned. Its body in the sand
socket for an eye
belly ripped spilling out a
tiny prehistoric beast.

A Ghost Story

I didn't believe
the ghosts had bones but she did:
ghost in a flowered sheet
waiting for someone she loved
could never remember who.

LOOK INSIDE!

There was an old lady who swallowed a horse.
She's dead of course.

When Andrea was 7 her sister stole a teddy bear pyjama case from Betty Preece's shop in The Arcade. To be sure she kept the secret, she gifted it to Andrea along with a threat. Andrea didn't want to fill the bear with clothes but she loved its face and yellow fur and the sound the Velcro made when she pulled it apart. She liked to put her hand inside the body but she worried that the bear was thin and didn't have the bulk to sit upright so she filled it with the secret notes she wrote in bed at night and her grandma's empty perfume bottle and the stone she saved from the tide and the lace from the perfect shoes that she'd outgrown. For years she refused to go to school. None of the adults thought to look in the bear; it would have shown them everything.

Auntie Irene says that cousin John got a tapeworm from stroking the sheep. The doctor gave him medicine and next day the worm came out with his poo and it was six foot long and white and writhing in the toilet but it had no head. Auntie Irene says it had snapped at the neck with its head still stuck inside so it will grow again like the garden worm mum accidentally chopped in half with a spade. Every time I see my cousin John I want to ask him if the tapeworm is still growing in his insides and every time he speaks to me I wonder will it come out of his mouth like words he didn't mean to say.

One day I watch a video by Mona Hatoum. It shows the journey of an endoscopic camera scanning her body then probing the tubes and cavities of her insides. It's loud: her amplified breath, gastric juices gurgling, beating heart. She's called it *Corps étranger* and the catalogue says that Mona Hatoum is interested in trespass and surveillance. I think of the secret body, a stranger in familiar clothes. I think of me and Debbie Watson coming home from school. It's dusk. There's a man in the alley. His dark trousers and smart winter coat. The flash of his stiff pink dick in the fading light.

Andrea's father always peeled and sliced an apple, removing the core and arranging the segments nicely on a plate. Sometimes he sprinkled sugar. Andrea liked it this way. When she was thirteen, she fell in love with a boy who carried apples in his bag. She watched how he bit them, hungry and casual, how they disappeared in his beautiful mouth, how he discarded nothing. One day he offered one to her. They sat on the grass and ate together. Andrea's oesophagus felt thin and hard but she didn't care. Later Heather Killick said if you swallow the pip of an apple the chances are it will sow itself in your insides and a tree will grow. The branches will pierce your intestines and you'll die.

One day I ask the doctor if he thinks that I might soothe my sore insides if instead of seeing them as raging moorland fires and tight elastic bands I picture an underground warren with chambers occupied by little animals. In reply he tells me of the time he baby-sat a colleague's guinea pig that blended with the carpet where he'd let it roam, how he accidentally stood on it and yes of course it died.

Mum says Nancy Gardiner might still be alive if she'd spoken up when she found the lump. I don't know what she means and I'm too scared to ask but when it's time to leave my uncle's farm and I'm trying not to cry, the secret lump inside my throat is big and hard. It's aching my neck and jaw and eyes and I don't say a word to anyone.

Janet Bradley says she wants to be a nun. She reckons the noises in her belly are the angels trying to tell her what comes next. Her grandma says she needs to eat a decent breakfast and remember the Holy Maid of Kent who in 1553 was hanged for talk like that. I don't believe in angels but one day Janet Bradley's stomach says we shouldn't get on the bus so we don't then later on we find out that it crashed into a yellow truck on Albany Road. Thankfully no one was hurt.

One day I go for a colonoscopy and the doctor asks would I like to watch. *It's rather beautiful* he says. I squint at the screen and it isn't beautiful; it's everything in me I'd rather hide. When I tell this to Andrea she says it reminds her of watching herself as she watched the therapist watching her; the wrench in her gut as they laid her insides out on the horrible carpet. She says she badly wanted to be beautiful but she wasn't and oh the shame of it.

Peter B says he knows about spontaneous combustion; it's all to do with exothermic reaction, hydrocarbon and maybe coal. I'm not listening. I want to hear about Matilda Rooney who in 1885, alone in her kitchen, burst into flames and burned to death from the inside. All that was left were her feet. The kitchen was totally unharmed.

Aged 9, Andrea doesn't know about menstruation so when she sees the patch of blood spreading from the crotch of her mother's summer slacks, she's very afraid. They're having a picnic: Andrea and her mum and dad and her sort-of cousin Keith. She can't remember the field they're in but she knows that no one mentions the blood. Her mother's talking a bit too loud as she shells the hard-boiled eggs and pours tea from the flask. She keeps tugging the tail of her shirt. Andrea's legs go shaky. She knows that everything's falling out of her mother's insides and that this is very shameful and her mother will surely die. And Andrea knows the shame is worse than the dying and this is why nobody speaks of it or helps or cries.

One day I was sawn in half on stage. I couldn't see a thing but my stomach vibrated and I heard a gasp from the crowd so I wondered had the illusion gone awry. As I lay blindfolded across the bistro table an awful lot of things went through my mind but I'd rather not share them and though I'll never know how the trick was done, everyone clapped at the end and it goes without saying both ends of me are still alive and the scars on my abdomen are all from other times so this was certainly magic.

NOTES ON WATER

an audio text for two voices

Scan QR code to listen to the original BBC Radio 3 production
first broadcast in 2022 on BBC Sounds above or SoundCloud below.

I'm swimming in an artificial pool
inside a broken building.
The water is deep and brown
and full of wreckage:
a floating rusted can, papers,
swelling as they soak.
I'm out of my depth, weak
breaststroke turning to doggy paddle,
an ache in the shoulder and hips.

A pink balloon taps my face,
a flotilla of paper party cups, nothing
that will make a raft.
Beyond the water, flaked plaster,
smashed windows. Wires hang
from the walls. My sister
is kneeling in the rubble. She has
no idea how close I am to drowning.

In a small terraced house
a woman waits through a long night.
She boils a kettle, washes cups,
palms three tangerines
to see if she remembers how to juggle.

The living room's reflected in the yard –
a sideboard hovers on the tiny pond,
her piano juts across the lane.
She's out there too, standing in the hedge,
wonders is it her ghost that waits inside.

At 3am I wake thinking of the man
who will leave in winter. My gut is tight,
my head white noise. I'm dry.
I feel my way downstairs, fill the kettle
in the dark, not ready for electric light.
The water's force surprises me,
splashing the tiles, soaking my arm.
My feet ache on the slabs and I wonder
how anyone bears the cold of swimming
a freezing river, the going-in, the shock
on the belly, the whole body gasping.
I want to try it, want to see if it stops
my heart or snaps me wide awake.

Upstairs her man lies soaked in pain
but still, the doctor doesn't come.
2am. 4.30. 5.15. She phones again –
a busy night, they say. They're on their way.
She goes upstairs to sit with him

but it's easier to look at a photograph –
the one she'll decide to frame when he dies.
He's on a boat, all smiles, binoculars
around his neck, everything blue
and calm and bright.

That was the day they saw the dolphins
who surfaced, laughing, glided beside them
close enough to touch. A day
of unexpected Highland sun,
a kind of happiness and she wonders –

was it there even then? The start of a mass
in his gut? A stain? Did he feel dis-ease
as it pooled, streamed in his blood? Or was it later,
on Ardnamurchan, driving through pouring rain,
the day he slipped and fell in a storm of magnolia

blossom strewn like confetti on the muddy bank?
The day the deluge blocked the well and she searched
for buckets, found the brook, the stash of bottled water,
laughed because this really didn't matter –
then saw how he couldn't cope any more.

* * * *

There's a smiling boy in the car park,
little Noah, pouring rivers from a watering can.
He calls me out to see how his streams
gather speed as they make their way
down the sloping tarmac, forking as they catch
on grit. He starts another and another,
wills them to connect, thrills when they do.
I refill can after can and join him,
building settlements of broken stone.
Some become islands, some are flooded,
some survive the bursting riverbanks.
He builds a shop and we plan to make the islanders
a boat but Ben is driving away in a van
and he can't help it – he's flattening the houses,
everything is smeared and rerouted when he's gone.

Later she'd walked alone by the sea loch, felt
the slow drip of loss, wonders was that why
she made a list of everything she saw – to give
to him, to keep something from seeping away.

'bladderwort,' she wrote
'white driftwood'
'flowers that might be meadow cranesbill'
'bits of wood.'

27

She couldn't stop –

'a Tennant's lager can, marsh marigold in clumps, 8 oyster-catchers, 14 adult sheep, 9 lambs, a broken rowing boat, a pair of dark-coloured ducks with 6 young, a crow, ringed plovers (5), red plastic – might be from a child's spade, dead crab, a herring gull, sheep's wool, the remains of a fire, 4 black-headed gulls, a plastic shoe (green), campion, plastic bottles (3), seawort, marram grass, a length of rusted metal chain, thousands of stones, 2 plastic bags, some shells, a rock, an orange rope, moss, gorse, wet grass (muddy), rock samphire, blue plastic piping, a broken pint glass (partly buried), sudden gathering of terns, a lot of seaweed – mainly knotted wrack and kelp, gritty sand, a gang of Canada geese, unexpected, round a bend'

and she took photographs for him –

the wader she couldn't identify

the perfect reflection of a sheep

the evening light on the loch after rain

the view from the opposite shore

and she saw how they didn't interest him,
how they all looked the same.

Flood. The whole town smeared, rerouted – floating cars on Albert Street, St George's Square an artificial lake, a drunken slap on a cheek, and the soaking books in supermarket trolleys, toxic slime on shovels, shoes, between the floorboards, up the walls. The drenched

and the nowhere-to-go and the lost-the-lot and don't
say it's almost beautiful the way the burst banks
remade the woods, don't say that a flooded cinema's
romantic.   So many carpets on the pavements. So
many fridges, sofas, Christmas trees. Open the door
and the hall's in the cellar, open the door and the TV's
caked in slime. There's a man in tears in the road with
his dog on his shoulders, looking at his half-submerged
front door. Next day the fucking sightseers blocking
the streets.

* * * *

Today the water sings. Today I walk the bank
with someone else's dog on a lead.
And it's like the river's saying *Yes?*
An ordinary day. Nothing doing here.
I watch a wagtail wagging stone to stone,
even the living-statue heron's there,
powdered grey, and I ask the dog
if we should give it a coin for its trouble.
There's a sycamore down and some branches
on the path but nothing like the fallen army
ripped apart that day in Ardnamurchan,
that defeated battlefield of trees
enough to make you weep. Then the dog
says *flow* and I say *fucking hippy dog*
and the river says
I'm thinking of the man who will leave in winter.

I am thinking of David Nash's *Wooden Boulder*,
that great ball of oak, slipping downstream,
stuttering for months, coming to rest
in the estuary until the heavy rains, high tides,
dislodge it again and again and it's gone.

29

I am thinking of David Nash gently searching
for years, how he said *It hasn't vanished.*
I just can't see it.

And the dog says *That'll do. Think that.*
Hasn't disappeared. You just can't see it.

> These days she can't bear the shower
> assaulting her skin, so she lies in the bath
> for hours, lets water out, refreshes it
> with hot until she nearly scalds.
> She thinks of how the wetness makes
> her fingers look like his, the puckered
> contours, knuckles pouched, but when
> she touches her thumb to her middle finger
> she hears a squelch, liquid
> moving underneath her flesh.
> And she wonders how half his body is water,
> even now as he desiccates.

* * * *

On the far side of the artificial pool
my sister is kneeling in the rubble
talking to an empty window frame,
talking to the wire that hangs from the wall,
telling the tale of a woman who walked her dog
beside a river that was fast and high.

The dog jumped in my sister tells the window frame,
was swept away. The woman followed the river
for miles, running and driving and shouting
for strangers to help her search for the dog
but no one found it, ever.

30

Lighten up I say to my sister, mouth full
of rusty water, grasping a paper party cup,
a pink balloon.

In just seven weeks he goes
from coffee and wine
to peppermint tea
to tiny fruits
to water
on a spoon
to this —
the last of the nights and days
when she holds his parched hand,
moistens his lips with balm, cups
a tiny glass to him
but he chokes on a sip
and the beautiful nurse says
just a drop on the tongue, like this
and when he opens his mouth for her fingertip
he's a fledgling.

I'm beside the river, drinking beer,
sunlight popping, rocks gargling, even the knot
of flies at the bridge is beautiful.
I want to jump, feel the liquid rush,
but I'm busy looking at maps to calculate
how long it would take for this particular stretch
to reach the man who will leave in winter.
And the answer is *forever* or, more brutally,
is never. The Calder joins the Aire at Castleford,
flows to the start of the Humber. *Useless.*
Derwent joined by the Wye at Rowsley – *Stop!*
This is stupid, pointless, childish, rather difficult.
Drink beer. Drift.

* * * *

There's an iPad on the floor of the broken building.
A *YouTube* man is teaching my sister to dance.

Start with your right foot he says *in front of your left.*
We're gonna hop on our left foot and then place down
our right.
Hop. 1. Pick up the left foot (and he's hopping)
place it down for two. 2. Pick up the right in front –

                            His feet are cold but he can't bear
                   the duvet, even a sheet, and so she looks
              for socks and finds the swimming shorts
                      he never wore and never will.
(After he dies she can't quite part with them).

                   He always said he hated swimming,
       still he would dive into pools and she remembers
          the violence of his splash, the wild front crawl,
               the way he shot underwater, up and out
                          in a single breath.

       – and my sister is up on her feet,
stepping and hopping and laughing and I laugh
too and whatever she's doing looks nothing like
a river dance.

                             * * * *

Then this.
This – before I have said goodbye to the man
who will leave in winter, before I can write
of the tall church spire that protrudes
from the lake in a drought, before I remember
the water diviner who found the line of liquid,
pure and running white beneath the old school hall.
This.

How to describe it?

A fault line that appeared in the ground in an instant,
patterned not unlike a river-bed and running fast
as Noah's little rivers, veining, widening, but dry as a bone?

A breach? Rubble falling down the gaps, a crack
that might have been a gun shot, fog of dust
from walls that crumbled almost silently?

> She thought of the hotel that fell into the sea,
> of the crockery and napkin rings still buried in the hill,
> the floating coat hangers, the reading spectacles
> a guest forgot to pack in his haste.

> She thought of the terrific speed of the fall

And as the pool fractured and the water
drained away, I thought of the stupid times
I had stayed in the bath after pulling the plug,
the heaviness in the limbs, the little shiver,
and I lay on stone with the paper cups and the pink
balloon, my gut tight, head white noise. Dry.
And I knew I must go deeper, close my eyes
and drop through the cleft,

> and she knew she must go deeper –

I knew I must find a river in the dark.

excerpt: "from notes on water"

* * * *

> Months after he dies she washes
> his clothes by hand, has no idea why,
> thinks perhaps she had wanted to bathe his body
> before they took it away, or is this a kind of

saying goodbye – to the smell of him,
to his skin, making sure he's no longer
there before she parts with him?
She hangs trousers, jumpers, jackets, shirts
on radiators, over rails, from the tops of doors,
until everywhere she turns, she sees him
all at once on different days, him
in a Pennine snowstorm, him in the blazing heat
of southern Spain. He stands behind her,
beside her, in front of a bookshelf, suddenly there
up close and she wants to bury her head
in his damp blue shirt but there's no chest
or shoulder and his arms are limp
and she can't tell is she taunted by the way that
everything hangs in the shape of him
those weeks before he died – so thin,
too weak for an embrace and she's overwhelmed
by his presence and by the absence of him.

end →

The water's force surprises me.

        A restless night, a storm,

the threat of flood.
I go deep into it, wear it,
feel the weight lighten me.

        At 8 am the ghostly wail of

the siren and by midday

I think I am in the river Cocytus

        streets are flowing,

steep roads surge.

or maybe this is just black water
running underneath an urban street.

Everything is river and the river is more than itself,
Carrying vehicles on its back, a fallen tree, trying to
drag its feet to calm the rage but it's too headstrong,
churning silt and gravel, spewing up a pushchair,
plastic shoe, dead jackdaw, bin. Everything is brown
and broken. Everything is wet.

She's out with the rest of the town in wellies,
rubber gloves, remembering the last flood,
how he'd cursed his lack of strength to bail and lift,
how he'd driven instead, delivered food to homes
that were drowned and she knows she should be glad
he isn't seeing this.

I can't see a thing
but somewhere far above, I know
my sister is kneeling, drawing
symbols in the dust
and the man who will leave in winter
slowly walks, a forked twig in his hands.
He knows what it takes to daylight a river
that runs underground; I know he is dowsing
for me. Soon he will find a stream
and follow it but –

She walks the woods but her old path
is gone. Perhaps that's why she turns for home,
makes a list of everything she's shifted since he died,
imagines him coming back to the tidy house:
new doorbell, missing folders, mended light.
Would she run from room to room like an excited child,
show him all she's rearranged? Or apologise?

Stop! This is pointless.

She waits for his car headlights,
shadow on the steps, key in the door.

Some rivers never meet.

She waits for his ghost,
(though she's not sure she believes
in ghosts), waits at least to dream of him
alive. But nothing comes.

She chips a tooth, the car breaks down,
the cats bring a dead wood pigeon in,
the cellar floor is soaked, invoices fall
through the door, she watches the news –
half the world underwater, the rest in flame.

He reaches the sea.

* * * *

Down here is jackdaw black,
blacker than blackout, blacker
than Vantablack and I am
cave fish, accidental troglomorph,
living underneath the world
with nothing but a raft of papers
breaking down in the wet.
I circle counter-clockwise, swim
until the fragments of my skull
change shape and I am asymmetrical,
losing colour, and my eyes are weak.

She dreams of strangers talking to her,
but she can't hear what they say,
dreams of shrouded cityscapes and faces
lost in fog, dreams she's almost blind
and swimming, in a fractured pool
in the bowels of an abandoned building.
Broken windows, rusted pipes. She's flailing,
breaststroke weak, can't see a thing,

Time slows in the black, folds in
on itself and disappears or perhaps
it's only time that's moving me.
I navigate by touch. I barely eat,

but somehow, somehow

still I feel these fins grow large
and though I can't see a thing
through these useless eyes,

she doesn't drown

they open and

she wakes.

I wake.

HAUNTS AND APPARITIONS

I've got you under my skin.
I've got you deep in the heart of me.

Nights I Squat

I hesitate to tell you but for years
I've been sheltering in your ear at night,
mostly quiet, curled between
the creak of tomatoes ripening,
the owl's occasional screech.
Sometimes you've heard me as rain
on the roof or an echo of the words
that swim inside your head,
keep you from sleep.

I apologise. I was the roar at 3am
that had you going down with a torch
and knife. I was the squeak you thought
was the old shed door. Don't be alarmed.
My song will not enchant you,
there's no need to tie yourself to the mast
to save your life. I have no wings,
don't play the harp. Think of me
as a touch of tinnitus that will pass.

Still, I can't forget the night when
half-awake you pressed your fingers
to your ear. Was it a minor itch, an ache?
Or did you know I was there?
You touched me and something whispered
in the dark. Did you hear?

Magic

Because these days
I can hardly tell
my left from right
my up from down
you might expect me
to believe in the demonic
pack of cards
think you can fool me
with a disappearing wrist
convince me
with that story
of the ghost inside a jar.
You can't.

But still
I think about the attic room
that scared me out of sleep
the mystery of the hinges
ripped from my little case
how I don't know
what touched my face
in the dark
or how I knew before I knew
the day my dad
two hundred miles away
had died. Unexpectedly.

* * * *

I saw him once
not an apparition
more a waking dream
at the zoo
in the house of butterflies
and I could hardly see
his old grey jacket
for the trembling
antennae and the wings
banded orange blues
all fluttering
the disappearing man
the man with wings
in his eyes
the remarkable
enchanted butterflies.

December 1979

Because we'd been in The Bull since 12
and now the light was fading and back
at halls a bulb had blown though Wendy
was singing Lou Reed we still took fright
when the phone rang out through the gloom.
I think it was Pam who answered
and later everyone said they knew I knew
(though I couldn't have possibly known)
because straight away I said *Dad*
then the porter on the end of the line said
your brother's here and I knew he wouldn't
have driven a hundred and fifty miles to say *hi*.

Today I put my bright-eyed dad in the car
with my brother. He's wearing his light grey
jacket and resting a map on his knee
though he always gets sick when he navigates.
Then I put them both at the door to my room
surprise surprise! Then we're in The Bull
my brother nursing a Theakston's
Dad a scotch and dry and later we weave
up the hill and though they don't really know
the words or the tune they sing
as we lean into one another
Such a perfect day I'm glad I spent it with you.

Three Hauntings

(after paintings by Peter Doig)

1 *Pelican*

You watched a man trying to drown a pelican in the sea,
watched him come ashore, the bird looping in his hand
as he wrung its neck. You said everything was strangely
quiet, that you were uncomfortable when he glared
as if to say *You shouldn't be witnessing this.*
You said you were thrilled.

It must be twenty years since the day I watched a man
dig for badgers in the wood, rifle slung, empty sacks,
terrier springing on the dead leaves. And though
I knew I could run if I had to, I was scared of his eyes
that seemed to say *I'm not afraid to shoot.*
Before today I've never mentioned this.

I gaze at your pelican man, painted again and again.
At first, he carried the bird but he's empty-handed now
and held in a flash of blue that might be light –
exposed I want to say – and the paint freed to run
from the canvas. Did it pool on the floor?
I can't stop staring.

2 *Girl in White with Trees*

She was eight. I think I left her up there
climbing through leaves – blue shoes,
yellow hair. It's dark now and she's bleached
much brighter than your average apparition.
I'd call her *My Childhood Ghost.*
Though there's hardly a face on her, I know
that cocked head, steady gaze that may be
recognition or defiance. I've seen it
in photographs, in the mirror. I want to climb
the tree, lit by the patterned Milky Way,
I want to climb to her, to know if that face
is smiling or in fear. I want to reach her
but I'm scared that she's malevolent
or I might fall or she might melt away.

3 *Man Dressed as Bat*

The head might be Batman but the body
is morphing into the ghost of butterfly
and if you hadn't labelled him I'd wonder

is he ectoplasm or just a kid in fancy dress,
arms out wide, a joke or maybe wraith
fading along with the light?

He's on the beach – I should have said –
infused with a sickly colouring of sand
and I'm afraid of those deep wings, thin legs,

afraid he might take flight. I don't even know
if he's looking at me or facing the veiled moon,
rainy sky and I'm a voyeur, awkward child

waiting to see, will he fold his wings,
will he walk into the waves as night falls
round his overlapping gauze, his frailty?

Missing

If they'd called my name I might have heard myself
but they didn't know my name. Or If we'd spread
across the high land to search for a heart as active
as the Katla volcano, I might have realised.
But no one dared to cross the unbridged river,
no one would climb the unpredictable slopes.

I was fire canyon, impassable glacier. I was the fall.

We barely spoke on the bus – it was not that kind of tour
and I was glad of it. Those days my own voice
sounded nothing much like me.
Lost in that fissure that ran through the landscape,
I'd turned to molten liquid long before. No wonder
I changed my clothes at least three times a day.

I didn't recognise myself.

We were looking for a woman in blue
when I wore red, looking for a quiet, bespectacled
spinster when I was roaring, my optic nerves burned out
in the heat. If they'd only asked,
I could have told them, we might have given up
the search, got back on the bus, discovered me.

The Vegetable Lamb of Tartary

Today the garden is turning to beech.
Through a winter of neglect its trees
have shed their load and now a thousand
tiny saplings sprout. If I don't pull them up
there'll be a forest here.
The sun is heavy, a change in the air, the door
to your old shed ajar to let two bees escape
and all along the terrace, neighbours' houses
open wide, their children's drawings
in the windows, names chalked onto slabs,
no other sign of human life.
The cats find a disposable glove that I mistook
for a clump of bluebells in the hedge.
They bring it home along with a mouse,
a crust of bread, a fly
and I wonder is this how we'll live, if we live
at all: scavenger-hunters, doors lying open
onto dark, the world returned to trees?

I go inside, try to write but I'm restless.
Through the window your old shirt dries
on the line, the one that I still wear to wrap
you round me but right now I wish it didn't hold
the shape of you. And there's the rocking chair
in the shed, the one that scared me
every night in the attic when I was a child
and I swore it rocked on its own, the creak of it
filling the dark like my grandma's breath
the week before she died.
I tune the radio, away from politicians
and their lies, away from *We'll Meet Again,*
You'll Never Walk Alone, find a choir singing
something beautiful that might be Bach
and I wish I could cry or laugh.

I'm trying to write about The Vegetable Lamb
of Tartary, the myth of a sheep that grew
as the fruit of a plant, connected to the stem
by an umbilical cord that allowed it to graze
nearby. When the greenery within its reach
was gone, both plant and sheep would die.
Perhaps I wish I could grow a sheep, or perhaps
I have – but I didn't mean to grow a sheep
that couldn't reach a meadow, couldn't spring
in this unseasonal air.
I imagine, for every beech tree shoot,
the woollen white of a new-born sprouting,
first like cotton-grass and then its bleat, plaintive
across the gardens as it searches for milk,
for ragged grass, finds a fly, a crust of bread,
blue glove in the hedge nearby.

like a tree

the white bark is shedding its layers
she picks at it
loves the feel of peeling
like separating tissue papers
or lifting a scab
she remembers the birch
growing out of the slabs
when she was a child
how it turned black at its base
the fissures and warts on its silverness

out here on the parched land
she wonders how anything grows
waits for catkins to hang like lambs' tails
waits for rain
she has gathered the fallen twigs
set a fire on the earth
beside her crappy tent
alone

he wouldn't walk with her
for fear of getting burnt he said
for the time of the blaze
in case she remembered
how to make a flame without a match
or startled him with her knack
of using stone to hold the heat

still
despite

yesterday he was suddenly there
searching for char

checking for embers
that might not have died
he stamped his heel at the pale ash
she showed him a can of water
for reassurance
told him how the birch tree
tolerates the dry

then he spoke of a silver man
whose back was blanched
from fire a field of snow
spoilt with knotted mounds
and ridged skin
he found a stick
and drew on the ground
the scarred back
of the silver man
and it looked like him
and it looked like a tree

The Possibility of Fog

(after Jaan Kaplinski)

If this long familiar road can turn to cataract,
my friend become invisible though he still stands
at my side, if the heifer can die from grazing
air and water as she stumbles to the barn,
if in a moment everything can muffle, everything
murmur and cling like apparitions in the night
though it's only 2pm, if I can be so suddenly
and spectacularly lost in the place I was born,
lost before there's even time to watch
the bowl of the valley fill with floss
(delicate muslin turning like those useless
curtains we used to wrap around ourselves
when we were young and drunk),
if cloud can fall to the ground then rise again
and there's the old oak that was gone
and the meadow grass and a spider's web
and the road all glittered with frost
and my friend beside me laughing
and someone has turned the volume up
and there's even a merlin high in the air –
if this is possible then maybe everything is possible.

Ten Signs of Possession

1 *Superhuman Strength*

My love
there is no doubt – today, with just one hand,
I could lift this house and everything in it,
carry the load to a field by a river
wherever you are. I'd take the motorway
for speed, my back straight, arms bearing
the weight of bricks and slate and wood
and every room and the bed and the bath
and all the books still alphabetical inside.
I'd shout *Wide Load!* as sharp blue lights
flashed warnings through my skin.
I'd be unearthed. The shock of touching me
would swerve a lorry, spark a nearside wing.
Carnage on the central reservation.
Queues for miles. Too bad. I'd be unstoppable,
coming through, carrying this house to you.

2 *Knowledge of Previously Unknown Languages or Speaking in Tongues (glossolalia).*

It starts in the butchers, asking for *huhn* instead of chicken, saying *dovidenia* for goodbye. In the street she shouts *fean skyld hva er galt med meg?* (which apparently means 'fuck's sake, what's wrong with me?'). The GP orders a brain scan, quotes some Scottish guy who woke from a coma speaking fluent Mandarin. What to say? Next day she's babbling, a language that doesn't exist or is maybe disallowed or dead. Could be Norn, Khazar or Semigallian, but the specialist writes *glossolalia* and the chemist (who's a Charismatic Christian) whispers *You're speaking the language of angels – there is no remedy.*

3 *Unnatural Body Movements*

When it says *movements*, is that like dance
or epilepsy? Or bowels, maybe, or a shifting womb?
And is *unnatural* like that woman who fell in love
with the Eiffel Tower, or the months I tried
to learn the balalaika? (I gave up on that.)

My body is brewing a storm, I must admit.
It keeps on leaving the house without me
and when I go out it often stays behind.
Then yesterday, when I saw you and we
weren't allowed to touch after all this time,
it tugged so hard that as you left, although
my head spun hard away from you,
my feet refused to say goodbye.

I told the man who sells olives on the market
how other heads had turned in the street
as my body separated into two. He said
he doubted passers-by would have known
if they should clap or call an ambulance.

Someone once wrote *mental perturbation*
but I don't think that counts, do you?

4 *Appearance of Wounds that Vanish as Quickly as They Appear*

A bruise where nothing knocked or held or pressed; heels
that blister as she lies on the unmade bed; above one eye the
bud of a puncture wound and a rash on her throat like a
spillage spreading now to her naked breast. Her neighbour
wants to cover her; the doctor tries to hold her head but she
shakes it free; every mark will be gone with the last of the
light and in any case this is, she says, the nearest she's ever
felt to being alive.

5 *Paranormal Capabilities*

I saw more doctors.
One said *telaesthesia*, one said
seeing things that just aren't there,
but I am *perceiving* you! Admittedly,
I can also taste your mind (I always do).
Divine. But, dearest heart,
that's not the half of it. These days
I'm lighting fires with my eyes,
I float to you and every day I lift
this pen and watch the letters
write themselves. I hardly recognise
a word – though every word is true.
Don't be afraid. I promise I will only use
no-hands to move the vase of feverfew
a little to the right so I may hear
your absent face and see your voice
ask what possesses me.
I thought you knew.

6 *Living Outside the Rules of Society*

It's true, she hasn't jumped the lights, gone off-grid or joined a circus, hasn't stolen sweets from children, left a battered sofa on the street. She's kept her clothes on in the Co-op, stayed off the grass, stood on the right, followed the recipe, even the rules of *World in Flames*. But just look at her, will you? No – actually – don't.

7 *Being Persistently Ill, Falling into Heavy Sleep and Vomiting Strange Objects*

They've called it gastroenteritis,
stress, exhaustion, hypochondria,
Covid, flu. No one's said
possession but they didn't hear
from the miniature child
lodged in my oesophagus,
they weren't in the room
the day I opened my mouth
and watched in the mirror
as a tiny boat navigated
the weir of my tongue.
And I was alone when I retched
and up came the bird
from that book you gave me –
one black wing in the toilet bowl,
the broken beak between my teeth.
I'm feeling wretched.
Might be dying of this.
Can anyone tell me – should I
anoint my skin with the grease
of a bear? Call a priest?

Troubled by a monkey in a petticoat, troubled by a shudder in the washing-up water, by the watch that she found in the freezer, by the curtains (their height, their sheen). Electricity. The bulbs in her house have exploded, she's static, sparking blue lines in the dark, buries her phone in a pot beside the rosemary but still it's sending messages she swears she didn't write. She holds her breath then talks of nothing else but breathing, calls her inhalation *him* (whoever *he* might be). Men in ties read her swollen files and mutter. No one will touch her.

Tie me to a post somebody,
saturate me.
Lure this out of me with terrible singing.
Then what?
Where will they put it?
How will they get it into the hen
or the old brown dog that roams the yard?
And if against the odds they somehow
ram it up an arse or down a throat,
then what?
Who'll wring the neck of the chicken?
Who'll throw the dog in a pit?

10 *Making Sounds and Movements Like an Animal*

Aaaarkkk
    Gruurder   Gruurder
        Kaah   Kaah   Kaah
            Yooooooouuuyoouuuyooouu

She jumps and though her arms are spread like wings she
doesn't fly. A disused quarry sprouting new growth. Men
running through the fields to reach her but she's all goat,
scaling the other side, over the lip and off. The consultant
says *at a gallop*, the boyish one with the clipboard mutters
crazy cow. She sheds her blouse, spins her skirt above her
head, reaches the river naked. A bloke with binoculars
reckons she's channelling the white-throated dipper; the
priest looks away, swears that the break in the clouds is a
sign. And though none of them say it, they want her tiny
form, pale flesh. But she's much too far away to reach, a
fawn splashing, jumping stones with the current and later
they'll have to agree – she looked ecstatic, heavenly.

Aftermath

And speaking of miracles,
today for just one hour
my body held itself upright,
was strong as – what – a sapling?

Once I grew a tree, so I know
a sapling's not robust
but it can bend before
it snaps in two and for a while

my body was springing back
like that and my tongue –
it woke up too, tapped
the roof of my mouth,

stroked my teeth
and my lips moved with it.
Words. A language
you and I both understand.

Admittedly, it didn't last.
I'm back on the slabstones now,
under the floral eiderdown
my grandma kept on the bed.

And you, you're still
behind my eyes, in every ache,
in every broken fingernail
but mostly, yes, behind my eyes.

But at least, for just that hour
we were both looking out, out
at the frosted window, low sun
resting its weight on the hill

and speaking of miracles – look –
a splash of palest green against
the wall, a brimstone butterfly,
alive, quiescent, out of the woods.

Untitled

One day, months after he dies, she goes for a walk around the house and she finds the broken elephant with its calf inside and the tiny model badger that she bought for him when the real ones stopped coming to the yard and the fossil of a fish a hundred million years old from Brazil. And she finds a photograph of him and then another in black and white. She goes outside and finds a stone by the pond and half a wooden peg that's fallen from the washing line and in the shed she finds a table and puts everything on it. Then she finds the day she dropped the elephant on the slabs and he wanted to throw it away and she said *don't*. She finds the very first night the badgers came and he got out of bed to join her in the freezing dark watching from the window and it was beautiful and she finds the fossil shop in Edinburgh and the time he travelled up alone to meet her there and she sees him from a high window, down in the courtyard in his pale blue shirt, waiting for her. And she finds the old door that's the same shade of blue and the one with a porch and the one with the patterned glass and the cottage door and then the stone is a stone from Ardnamurchan and she finds the rain that's there and the walk round the loch at dusk and there are no midges and she finds him sitting on the garden bench the day the sun came back and then the stone is Ullapool and she finds his shoes as they appeared beside her suddenly as she combed the sand and he lifts his arms to the light and the clothes peg is the way he puts up the washing line and carries the laundry basket over the grass and she finds his clothes among hers. And in the shed she finds the table clean and new in their old house, thirty years ago, the Christmas dinner on it, his purple cracker hat. And she leaves them – all the things on the table – leaves the shed, goes back to the house, walks round it, searching for everything she hasn't found.

Fantastic Voyage

I'm seven years old at the dentist, having a tooth extracted under gas. My face is clamped in a black rubber mask, body held down. I'm drowning in toxic air. As I go under, I shrink and before I know it I'm sucked into my own throat. Miniature me stands at the lip of the windpipe – or is this the tube that carries food? Ahead of me is stuff that looks like the carcasses in Mr Worsley's van on Earlsdon Street, livid and swaying and damp. But it's pulsating, so it isn't dead meat; it's Melanie Parker's pregnant gut at the swimming pool, the slugs my mother salted at the kitchen door. Inside the tube the beat is louder and something's breathing from a place I can't locate. I follow it. I follow it because I can, because, though I didn't ask for this, the thrill is more than the scare and shrunk is not the shrunk of less or withered, shrunk is not recoiled, belittled, not made light of but made light and so more possible. Moisture gleams on the walls. From far away a voice calls my name. I won't reply.

NOTES

Fantastic Voyage (9, 68) is a 1966 American science fiction film in which a submarine and its crew – a group of scientists – are shrunk to microscopic size in order to venture into the body of an injured scientist to repair damage to his brain. Screenplay by Harry Kleiner, adaptation by David Duncan. Based on a story by Otto Klement and Jerome Bixby, and novelised in 1966 by Isaac Asimov.

Takotsubo (10) refers to the Japanese name for an octopus pot which has a unique shape, resembling the left ventricle of the heart. The medical condition Takotsubo syndrome is sometimes called broken heart syndrome and is characterised by sudden and acute heart failure, usually affecting people who have experienced intense emotional distress.

A Ghost Story (10) draws on the 2017 film of the same name by David Lowery.

Notes on Water (23) was first published by Smith | Doorstop as a pamphlet of two long poems. This version of the text, an audio piece for two voices, was first broadcast in the series *Between the Ears* on BBC Radio 3, 10 April 2022. It was read by Amanda Dalton and Colette Bryce, with a soundscape by Laurence Nelson. The producer was Susan Roberts.

Nights I Squat (41) takes its title from a line in 'The Colossus' by Sylvia Plath.

Pelican (45) refers to the Peter Doig paintings *Pelican (Stag)* and his several versions of ***Pelican.***

Missing (48) was inspired by a true story first reported in various news articles in 2012.

The Possibility of Fog (53) was written in response to Jaan Kaplinski's 'The Possibility of Rain'.

Ten Signs of Possession (54) draws its subtitles from a range of Googled guides for spotting demonic possession. Handy!

ACKNOWLEDGEMENTS

Thanks to the editors and commissioners of the following publications and broadcasts where versions of some of these poems first appeared: T*he Poetry Review*, *PN Review*, BBC Radio 3, Smith|Doorstop, *The North*, *Acumen*, Arc Publications, Wenlock Poetry Festival Anthology.

Thanks to Sue Roberts for encouraging me to make a version of *Notes on Water* for audio broadcast, and to Colette Bryce and Laurence Nelson for making the project so special to me. Huge thanks every day to my very dear friends and family (where would I be without you?), to Nick Read, the 'Poety' club, Tony and Angela at Arc, and my special poetry friends: Peter and Ann Sansom, Jackie Kay, Clare Shaw, Alicia Stubbersfield, Carola Luther, Kim Moore, Anne Caldwell, Liz Almond and Maura Dooley.

And, of course, to wonderful Neil Astley and Bloodaxe. Thank you.

The epigraph to the section *Look Inside!* quotes from the children's song 'I Know an Old Lady' by Rose Bonne and Alan Mills. The epigraph to the section *Haunts and Apparitions* quotes from the 1936 song 'I've Got You Under My Skin' by Cole Porter.

The front cover shows 'Entering a gland cave. Ideal landscape picture of the microscopic structure of a man's body', an illustration by Arthur Schmitson from Dr Fritz Kahn, *Das Leben des Menschen*, Vol. II (Stuttgart: Franckh/Kosmos, 1924), www.fritz-kahn.com

Fantastic Voyage is dedicated to the memory of David Groves.